The Adventures of Odysseus

The Lotus-Eaters

The city of Troy was in flames.

Odysseus looked back, and laughed.

For ten bitter years the Greek army had laid siege to the city. Now at last they had done what they came to do. The walls of Troy, built by the god Poseidon himself, were tumbled to the ground. Paris, Prince of Troy, who had dared to steal away the beautiful Helen from King Menelaus, was dead. Now they could go home.

It was not much, perhaps, Odysseus's home. Ithaca – a poor, bare, low-lying island far out to the west; the island of the setting sun. But every man loves the land where he is born, and no place on earth was dearer to Odysseus than Ithaca. For all those years that the Greeks had warred against Troy, his heart was yearning for his home.

The soil of Ithaca may be thin and starved, but it grows true sons. Odysseus had left one behind: Telemachus. He thought often of his son and his wife Penelope, and longed to be with them.

In truth, he had never wanted to leave them. What did he care if Paris had taken a fancy to Menelaus's wife Helen? When Agamemnon, Menelaus's brother, who led the Greek army against Troy, came to collect Odysseus to join the expedition, he had pretended to be mad. He yoked a horse and a bull together to plough the seashore, and sow it with salt. But they pushed his son Telemachus into his path. Odysseus swerved to avoid him, and they saw through the act.

"Odysseus, you shall plan for us," said King Agamemnon. "For your cunning may win where strength fails."

Cunning, indeed, was needed, where the strength and bravery of the two sides was so finely balanced. It was Odysseus who came up with the plan to deceive the Trojans into opening their city gates, so letting the

finest Greek soldiers into the city, concealed in a wooden horse. Then Troy was put to the fire and the sword.

Of all the leaders of the Greeks, Odysseus was the most eager to be on his way. He called his men to him, and they set sail, while the sky behind them still burned red.

But bad luck was with them from the start. Great Zeus, who wields the thunder and lightning, sent such storms that their ships bucked and plunged in the waves like frightened horses. The rain scoured all colour from the world, until they could not tell the sea from the sky. The wind tore their sails to shreds. There was nothing they could do but pull for shore.

There they lay, weary and sick at heart, for two days and nights while the storm blew itself out. On the third day, they set sail once more, only to be caught by fierce currents that pulled them far off course. They were dragged south by the relentless wind and waves for ten whole days, until at last they reached land.

They went ashore and soon found fresh water. Odysseus sent a party of men inland, to find out who lived in this hot far-off country.

None of them returned.

At last Odysseus himself went in search of them. In a clearing, he found one of his men. He was lying on his back, humming a tune. Odysseus recognized the melody; it was an old Ithacan lullaby, such as every mother croons to her baby.

The man hardly seemed to recognize Odysseus. Instead he held out some fruit, saying, "Here, have some." His voice was slurred, and juice from the ripe fruit was dribbling down his chin.

Odysseus slapped his cheek to bring him round. Little by little, the story came out. This was the land of the Lotus-Eaters – so-called because their only food was the honeyed lotus fruit. They had offered their fruit to Odysseus's men. Whoever tasted it once, lived only to taste it again.

Odysseus tried to reason with the man. "Don't you want to come home?" he asked.

"I'm already home," the man mumbled, his mouth full of fruit. He began to slip once more into his waking dream, and nothing Odysseus said could stir him from it.

Odysseus returned to the ships and fetched more men, cautioning them not to eat the lotus fruit. One by one, they dragged their blank-eyed, smiling companions back to the ships. They tied them up, and fled from that deadly land, where men are trapped by the lotus fruit in a trance of childhood.

As the oars dipped once more into the whitening sea, they tried to shut their ears to the piteous cries of those men who had eaten the lotus fruit.

In the Cave of the Cyclops

Odysseus and his men sailed on, sad and weary, until they came to the country of the Cyclopes. These huge, fierce beings have only one eye right in the centre of their foreheads. They do no work, relying instead on the goodwill of Zeus, whose thunderbolts they make. So, although they neither plough nor sow, still their crops grow. They live in caves high in the hills, and each of them makes his own laws.

The crews beached the boats in a fine harbour, close to a spring of fresh water and a grove of black poplars. They slaughtered some goats, and ate and drank, then slept at ease in this delightful spot.

When the first flush of dawn was in the sky, Odysseus picked twelve of his men and set out to explore. They climbed until they came to a cave, with a courtyard of wood and stone. It was clearly the home of some shepherd, for there were sheep and goats in pens, and also many huge cheeses in baskets.

"Let us take as many of these cheeses as we can carry, drive the animals on to the boats, and set sail before this shepherd returns," said Polites, one of Odysseus's most trusted companions. "From the looks of it, he must be a giant."

But Odysseus replied, "No, let us wait, and greet him when he returns from his pastures. He may be master of all this land, and if he knows what is due from host to guest, will give us gifts."

So they made themselves at home in the Cyclops's cave. They lit a fire and killed a sheep. After they had offered the gods the portion due to them, they ate. At last they heard the heavy tread of the Cyclops, whose name was Polyphemus. From a distance, he looked more like some vast mountain crag than flesh and blood. Their courage failed, and they hid in a dark corner of the cave, meaning to creep out when they could.

But when Polyphemus came home, driving his flocks and carrying a huge bundle of wood to make a fire, he closed the entrance behind him with an enormous boulder, so big that you couldn't shift it with twenty four-wheeled wagons. Then he settled down to milk the sheep and goats.

Something troubled the Cyclops at his work: a strange scent. He began to sniff the air. Searching the cave, he soon discovered Odysseus and his men, cowering in the corner.

"Who are you, and where do you come from?" he roared.

"We are Greeks, come from the sack of Troy," said Odysseus. "Show us, we beg, the hospitality due to wayfaring guests, as you respect the gods. For Zeus himself looks after travellers."

"And I look after myself," replied Polyphemus. "We Cyclopes do not fear the gods, for we are as strong as they are. Nevertheless I may choose to spare you. Tell me, how did you come here? Did my father Poseidon allow you to travel freely over the waves? Is your ship moored nearby?"

Odysseus, guessing that the giant would destroy their ships and murder the crews, replied, "Our ship was dashed against the rocks by great Poseidon and sank. My companions and I are the only survivors."

Polyphemus asked no further questions. Instead he reached down and plucked two men from the huddled group. He swung them by the ankles and dashed their brains out against the cave wall. Then he tore them limb from limb and devoured them raw, like a ravening animal. The others looked on in terror and dismay. Polyphemus washed his meal down with milk, and lay down to sleep.

As the Cyclops lay snoring on the floor, Elpenor, the youngest of Odysseus's men, urged Odysseus to kill him. "Slide your sword in between his ribs, just there! That should finish him off."

"It would finish us off too", replied Odysseus, "for how could we escape? Only the Cyclops is strong enough to budge the rock that seals us in here. No, we must wait and see what the new day brings."

At dawn, Polyphemus rose, and made a gruesome breakfast from two more of Odysseus's companions. He gathered his flocks and set out for the pastures, closing the rock door behind him. Odysseus and the remaining eight men were left to tremble in the cave, waiting for nightfall and the return of the Cyclops.

At last Odysseus spoke. "It may be that this Cyclops will eat us all, and that our only choice is between a swift or a slow death. But it may be that we can fool this giant. I have with me a goatskin full of dark red wine, given me by the priest of Apollo. This wine is so potent that it should be diluted with twenty parts of spring water. I shall offer it to the Cyclops tonight, and if he drinks he will fall into a fuddled sleep. Then we must make our move."

Polyphemus had left a great cudgel of olivewood lying in the cave, so big it could have served as the mast of a ship. Odysseus cut off a length of this, and sharpened the end with his sword. Then he and his men laid it in the ashes of the fire to harden, and finally they hid it out of sight.

Polyphemus returned, and again drove his flocks into the cave, closing the entrance behind him.

The Cyclops gorged himself once more on human flesh, and then sat down to drink some milk. Odysseus went up to him, saying, "Cyclops! You have caused my companions to drink the black wine of death. If you are to feast on men's flesh, you should at least send them on their way with honour. I have here a goatskin of fine wine, which I had brought to you as a gift. Let me pour you a bowlful."

The Cyclops drained the bowl in a single swig. Wiping his great blubbery lips, he said, "Tell me your name, little man, for I wish to make you a present in return for this wine. And pour me some more."

Three times Odysseus filled the bowl; three times the Cyclops drank it down. At last, the fumes from the wine began to fog his head. And then Odysseus said, "You ask my name, and I will tell you. It is Nobody."

"Well, Nobody, I will eat you last. That is my gift to you," replied Polyphemus. As the wine overcame him, he sank to the floor. His great head lolled to one side, and as sleep tugged him under, he belched forth a vile mouthful of wine and human flesh.

Odysseus and his men took the stake that they had made out of olivewood, and laid it in the fire until it was red hot. Begging courage of the gods, four of the men took the stake and plunged it into the giant's single eye. Odysseus, above, twisted it to and fro to drill it home. The eye bubbled and hissed with a sound like a smith tempering iron in cold water.

Polyphemus awoke shrieking in agony. He plucked the stake from his forehead, and hit out wildly, but Odysseus and his men could easily dodge the blind, blundering giant.

Polyphemus's screams resounded through the hills, waking the other Cyclopes in their high caves. They all rushed to help him. When they arrived outside his cave, they called, "What is the matter? Who is attacking you?"

And Polyphemus replied. "Nobody is attacking me. Nobody has tried to kill me."

The other Cyclopes were puzzled by this answer. But every time they asked Polyphemus who was to blame, he just wailed, "Nobody!"

"If nobody is attacking you, there is nothing we can do. You must ask your father Poseidon for help, if you are suffering some torment of the gods." And the Cyclopes went away.

Polyphemus groped around the cave for Odysseus and his men, but he could not catch them. So he pushed the boulder away from the entrance, and sat there himself, with his great hands outstretched to catch anyone trying to escape.

When dawn came, the sheep began to file out of the cave, as they were accustomed to do, and Polyphemus felt each one as it passed. But crafty Odysseus had tied them together in groups of three, so that a man could cling beneath the belly of the middle one and go undetected. And so his six remaining companions escaped from the cave.

When it was Odysseus's turn, there was only one ram left – a big, fat creature that was the best in all the flock. Odysseus clutched the shaggy fleece tightly and, with his face pressed to its rank-smelling belly, sent it walking towards the giant.

As it passed, Polyphemus hugged it close to him. "It's you, my beauty," he said. "Normally you are the proudest of all, and the first to leave the cave. Today you have lingered, out of sadness for your master. But I promise you, Nobody shall never escape me. Now, join your fellows in the meadow." And he let the ram go.

Once clear of the cave, Odysseus and his men drove the sheep down to the ships, and made haste to put out to sea, knowing that the Cyclopes made no boats and could not follow them on to the salt waves.

When they were the length of a man's shout from the shore, Odysseus cried, "Cyclops! Are you listening? It is I, Nobody! You scoffed at Zeus, and at the hospitality due to a guest. Now you must suffer for your evil ways."

At this the giant was so outraged that he hurled the massive boulder from the cave entrance at the ship. It landed in the sea with such a tremendous crash that the waves from it drove the ship back on to the shore.

As they rowed frantically out to sea again, Elpenor pleaded with Odysseus not to anger the Cyclops further. "Next time," he said, "he may aim better." But Odysseus was too proud to remain silent.

"Cyclops!" he shouted. "If anyone asks who blinded you, tell them it was Odysseus, Prince of Ithaca. It was my wits that breached the walls of Troy, though they were built by Poseidon himself, and it was I who made a fool of you."

Polyphemus let out a terrible groan. "It is my fate that this has happened. A wise man foretold I would lose my sight at the hands of Odysseus. But I thought Odysseus would be a great hero, strong and tall, not a puny weakling like you." Then he stretched out his arms towards the sea, calling, "Great Poseidon, Earthshaker, Lord of the Waves, hear me! If I am your son, and if you are my father, grant me this. May Odysseus never see his home again, or, if he does, let him come alone and friendless to a house of trouble and sorrow."

That was his prayer, and Poseidon heard it.

Then Polyphemus threw another great rock. This one fell just short of the ship, and its waves sent Odysseus and his men out to sea, to join the rest of the ships. There, Odysseus sacrificed the ram on which he had escaped, and prayed to Zeus for his help. But Zeus would do nothing to turn aside the anger of his brother Poseidon.

Goddess of Enchantment

Next Odysseus and his ships came to the island home of Aeolus, who is the warden of the winds. His island floats on the surface of the sea, and all around it is a wall of bronze. Aeolus lives there with his wife and twelve children: six sons and six daughters, who are married to one another. They spend all their time feasting.

For a whole month Aeolus entertained Odysseus and his men, and questioned them closely about the fall of Troy. At last, Odysseus asked Aeolus for his help on the journey home. "Without it, we will never see Ithaca again, for the gods are against us."

Aeolus gave Odysseus an ox-hide bag tied with a silver cord. In it were all the winds, to be let out as they were needed, except for the west wind, which Aeolus commanded to give Odysseus safe passage home.

At first, all went well. After nine days and nine nights, the shore of Ithaca came into sight. Odysseus, who had been keeping lookout all this time, fell asleep, sure that his long journey was nearly over. His crew began to mutter and whisper among themselves.

"He's coming home rich enough," said one.

"Aye," said another. "He has a shipful of spoils from Troy, while we have nothing."

"And now he has this bag full of gold and silver from Aeolus," said another.

"Let's open it," said the first.

And so the foolish, greedy men undid the silver cord around the ox-hide bag, and let out the winds.

At once a fierce tempest arose, buffeting the ships with merciless fury.

One by one, they foundered. They sank to the bottom of the sea, and the waves closed over them.

Soon only Odysseus's ship was left. The warring winds blew it all the way back to Aeolus's island.

He greeted Odysseus with amazement. "What are you doing back here?" he asked. "Did I not give you command of the winds to see you safely home?"

"You did," answered Odysseus, "but my companions betrayed me. They opened the ox-hide bag, and let loose the tempest. I beg you, gather the winds together again, so that I can go home."

"The gods are truly against you," said Aeolus, "and I cannot help you again. Go!"

Odysseus, heavy at heart, turned once more to the open sea. No friendly wind filled his sails this time; instead, the men had to pull on the oars against both wind and wave. And all the time they knew, no matter what course they steered, that Poseidon was waiting for them.

Odysseus and his men eventually made landfall off the island of Aeaea, the home of Circe, goddess of enchantment.

When they had beached the ship, Odysseus climbed a nearby hill to see what could be seen. As he stood gazing over the island, a stag crossed his path, on its way to drink from the river. Odysseus flung his spear and killed it.

"Men," he cried, "our luck is with us once again. Come, let us feast, and tomorrow we shall explore the island."

Next day, Odysseus divided his crew into two parties. He commanded the first, and his cousin Eurylochus, the second. They drew lots as to who should go first, and Eurylochus won. So he and twenty-two men set off inland.

Before long they came to Circe's palace. It stood in a clearing in the woodland and was built of stone. Wild creatures such as lions and wolves roamed outside it, but Circe's power was so great that they did not attack the men, but fawned on them like dogs.

When the party came to the doors of the palace they could hear Circe inside, singing in a lovely lilting voice as she worked at her loom, weaving such dazzling gossamer cloth as goddesses make.

Then Polites said, "There is a woman in the house, singing as she weaves. The whole building rings with the echoes of her voice. Come, let us go in." They entered, with no suspicion in their hearts. Only Eurylochus waited outside, ill at ease.

The goddess welcomed them. She served them wine and sweetmeats, mixing in them drugs that made them forget their country and their loved ones, and long only to serve Circe the goddess of enchantment. Then she touched each of them lightly with her rod, and as she did they turned into bristly, snuffling swine. Their minds remained the minds of men, but when they tried to cry for help, only a grunt came out.

Eurylochus saw it all, and ran back to the ship with the terrible news. The men wanted to sail at once, abandoning Polites and the others but Odysseus would not leave them.

As he made his way to Circe's palace, Odysseus met Hermes the messenger god, with his golden wand and gold-winged sandals. He looked like a boy on the edge of manhood, with the first soft down still on his upper lip. Nevertheless, Odysseus bowed low, knowing he was in the presence of a god.

"Unlucky man," said Hermes. "You can never free your companions from Circe's power. But wait! Here grows a herb that will keep you safe from her witch's potions. It is called *moly*, and while you carry it no harm can come to you.

"Circe will try to drug you. When she touches you with her rod, you must draw your sword as if to strike her. Then she will beg you to be her lover, and you must agree, for she is a goddess. But first make her swear to do you no harm; otherwise, she may steal away your courage and manhood as you lie naked in her bed."

Hermes departed, and Odysseus carried on his way to Circe's palace. When he reached the door he cried out to be let in. Circe welcomed him, ushered him to a chair, and handed him a golden goblet in which she had mixed her magic potion.

When he had drunk, she touched him with her rod, saying, "Now, be off to the pigsty and lie down with your friends." But he remained a man.

He drew his sword and raised it high as if to strike her dead. Circe fell to her knees, and spoke in pleading tones. "Who are you? How is it you can resist my magic? Only one man could have so strong a heart: Odysseus. If you are he, sheathe your sword, and come with me to my bed. There, we may learn to trust one another."

Odysseus answered. "How can I trust you, when you have turned my men into swine? Promise to free them, and to do me no further harm, and I will lie with you willingly."

The goddess gave her promise. She opened the door of the sty, and Polites and the others came trotting out, looking just like full-grown swine. Circe smeared an ointment on them, and their bristles fell away, their snouts receded, and their limbs lengthened. Soon they were standing upright once again, looking younger and more handsome than before.

Then, as Circe's handmaidens prepared her bedchamber, Odysseus went back to the ship, to tell Eurylochus and the others the news. The men would not believe him, and wanted to put straight to sea, but Odysseus told them, "I have given my word to a goddess, and I cannot break it."

When they reached the palace, Circe welcomed them. "Put aside your cares," she said. "Eat, drink, and be merry." For a year, Odysseus's men feasted, while Odysseus kept loving company with the goddess, who bore him a son, Telegonus.

At last, however, they grew homesick, and Odysseus begged Circe to help them to go back to Ithaca.

"You have offended the most powerful of the gods," said Circe, "and I cannot help you. If you want to return to your home, you must ask advice from the wisest of all, the blind seer Teiresias."

"But Teiresias is dead," said Odysseus.

"Yes, you must venture into Hades itself to speak with him It will be worth the journey, for while the rest of the dead are mere flitting shadows, Teiresias keeps his wits about him still. He alone can tell you what your future holds."

"Who will pilot me on such a voyage?" asked Odysseus. "No sailor has ever undertaken the dark journey to the house of death."

"Do not worry," she replied. "Just hoist your white sail, and the north wind will carry you where you wish to go. Once you have passed the River of Ocean, you will come to the coast of Hades, with its black and blighted trees. There you must leave your ship, and walk into the land of death. When you come to a rock where two rivers meet, dig a trench, and fill it with milk and honey. Add sweet wine, then water, and sprinkle barley-meal upon it. Then, with heartfelt prayers, you must promise that on your return to Ithaca you will make sacrifices to the dead, and to Teiresias especially.

"You must take a ram and a ewe, and sacrifice them. The numberless hordes of the dead will swarm at the scent of blood, but you must hold them back with your sword, until Teiresias arrives. He will answer all your questions."

Odysseus gathered his men, and returned to the ship. But one did not come with them. Young Elpenor, having drunk too much wine, was lying asleep on the palace roof. Hearing his companions calling for him, he leapt up, lost his footing, plummeted to the ground, and broke his neck.

Odysseus meanwhile spoke to his men. "No doubt you think we are heading for home. But we are not. Our destination is Hades where the goddess has told me to seek the advice of the seer Teiresias."

And the men took to sea once more.

The Voyage to Hades

Odysseus and his crew did not have to touch the oars as their ship carried them to the dread land of death. Circe's breeze filled the sail to speed them across the darkening sea to the very spot she had described.

There, Odysseus poured out milk and honey, sweet wine, and water for the dead, and promised them a sacrifice when he should return to Ithaca. With many prayers and invocations, he slaughtered the ram and the ewe, and dark blood filled the trench.

Ghosts flocked to the place of sacrifice, drawn by the vital energy still pulsing from the hot blood. Old men, young girls, battle heroes, peasants – their shades clamoured and jostled about the trench.

At the head of the throng was the ghost of Elpenor.

Odysseus wept to see him in the land of gloom. "We sailed with all speed," he said, "but you have outstripped us."

However, Odysseus would not let any of the shades feast on the blood, until blind Teiresias came, leaning on his golden staff.

"Draw back and let me drink." said Teiresias, "Then I will reveal your future to you."

Odysseus put up his sword, and Teiresias bent to the steaming blood. Then he spoke.

"Prince Odysseus, you have come from the sunlight into the land of shadow, in order to learn your fate. So listen.

"You seek a safe passage home, but this will not be easy. For you have offended the Earthshaker, Poseidon. First, your cunning brought down the walls of Troy, that Poseidon himself had set up. Second, you have blinded his son, the Cyclops Polyphemus.

"You cannot hope to escape the anger of the gods completely. But if you are careful, you and your companions may yet come safely home.

"Be warned, if you arouse the wrath of the gods once more, the reward will be death and misery. If you return home at all it will be late, and alone. You must hope it is not too late. For even now, suitors from many lands are arriving at your palace, and wooing your wife Penelope with fine gifts and finer words. Your son Telemachus is still a boy. How can he protect her?"

Odysseus answered, "I will heed your words. Whatever may befall, I shall not give up hope. When he was still a child, my son Telemachus fell from a fisherman's boat into the salt sea, yet he was not lost. A dolphin carried him on its back safe to shore; that is why the seal on my ring shows a leaping dolphin. In the same way, surely the gods that weave my fate will bring me safely home at last."

After that, Odysseus let each of the shades, one by one, feed on his sacrifice. And as they did so, they seemed to take on substance, and remember themselves again.

Odysseus was stricken to see his mother, Anticleia, among them. "Mother!" he cried. "Tell me, what brought you to this dim land?"

"It was longing for you, my son," she replied.

Odysseus reached across the trench to comfort her. Three times he tried to clasp her, but it was like embracing mist.

Then came the ghost of Agamemnon, who had led the army against Troy. Odysseus asked him, "Did you, too, arouse the anger of Poseidon on your journey home?"

"No." replied Agamemnon. "I sailed home safely, longing for my wife, Clytemnestra. But she and her lover cut me down with an axe as I came from my bath. May the gods save you from such a homecoming, friend."

Odysseus questioned all who came, and they told him their stories. Some still hugged their envies and spites to them like precious treasures. Some remembered golden days and tender words. But none had thought for the future, except the blind seer Teiresias.

The Song of the Sirens

From Hades, Odysseus returned to Aeaea, to thank Circe, and to bury the body of Elpenor, as his ghost had requested.

"Welcome, brave men," she greeted them. "You have faced death undaunted. For most, it is enough to meet death once in a lifetime, but you are fated to do so twice. But now, forget murky Hades. Eat and drink, and in the morning you shall set sail."

Odysseus and his men were glad to be back in the world of light and laughter, and spent that evening celebrating. Next day, Circe bade them farewell, with some last words of advice for Odysseus.

"You must sail past the island of the Sirens. They bewitch passing sailors with their beautiful singing; if you sail too close to them, you will fall under their spell, and that will be the end of you. For though they seem from the sea like lovely maidens, once they have lured you ashore they will turn into hag-like birds of prey. Their island is littered with the bones of men they have trapped and devoured.

"Once safely past the Sirens, more dangers await you. You must choose between two terrible routes. The first is overshadowed by great rocks, known as the Wanderers, because they do not stay still, but clash together, and seem to take pleasure in smashing ships into pieces. Only Jason and the Argonauts have ever passed that way in safety, and that was with the help of the goddess Hera.

"The other route is bounded on one side by cliffs so high that you cannot see the sky above them. Halfway up these cliffs is a dingy cave, in which the monster Scylla lives. Her cry will not frighten you; it is no more worrying than a puppy's yelp. But if you see her you will not forget her. She has twelve dangling feet, and six long necks, each topped with a grisly head, each with three rows of evil teeth. From her cave she fishes in the roaring sea below, scooping out dolphins and sharks and other sea-beasts. She feasts greedily with all her heads from the deck of any passing ship, glutting herself on death.

"On the other side, the cliff is lower. A fig-tree grows upon it, but do not steer beneath its shady boughs. For there Charybdis lurks. Three times a day she sucks the dark waters down, then jets them back in a hideous fountain. If you are caught by her, there is no hope for you. Better to steer by Scylla, and lose six men, than for all to perish in the maw of Charybdis."

"Could we not slay these monsters?" asked Odysseus.

"Don't be a fool," replied Circe. "These are deathless creatures, beyond your strength and understanding."

Odysseus set sail once again, worrying about how best to deal with the perils ahead.

As they neared the island of the Sirens, he told his men of the dangers facing them. "We must not listen to the Sirens' song," he said, "or we shall be lost. You must block your ears with soft wax, so that you cannot hear." But Odysseus himself could not pass by the fabled island without hearing the song that was so beautiful it could lure men to their deaths. Again heeding Circe's words, he told his men to lash him to the mast, and made them promise not to release him, even if he commanded them to.

When they drew near to the island, the wind dropped. All was calm and hushed. And into that hush dripped the honeyed notes of the Sirens' song – a song of longing and welcome, of promise and delight. To listen to it was both a rapture and a torment. Odysseus begged and pleaded with his crew to set him free, so that he could follow the song to its source, but they would not, and only bound him tighter to the mast.

Once past the Sirens' isle, Odysseus chose to take the route between Scylla and Charybdis, knowing that no friendly god would speed his ship past the dreadful Wanderers. Soon he could see ahead the crash and spray of the waters. It was a frightening sight, and the roaring of the sea beneath Scylla's cave, together with the low belching sound as Charybdis sucked down the waters and spewed them out again, drained the courage from the rowers, who let their oars dip into the water.

Odysseus urged them, "Be brave! This is no worse than when we were